from me, to you

love poems
by katherine j zumpano

for Tre. I love you endlessly.

<u>poems</u>

in which you take me to the cascades for the first time

in which we watch my words burn

in which our new year's kiss is at 3pm

in which I bake banana bread as a gift

in which you travel by plane for the first time

in which we get drunk in a las vegas speakeasy

in which we sit by the campfire all night

in which you decide to quit your job

in which I cry at the boygenius concert

in which I compose a love letter

in which you take me to the cascades for the first time

diablo lake shines under the july sun, a gemstone
in the north cascades. the mountain range beyond
reflects off the lake's surface. deep green trees inverted
against water so blue   it must be the sky.
I hadn't known something so beautiful
existed here. this is the first summer I don't long
for the california coast. I am finding
comfort here, one beautiful thing
at a time. I am new to washington,
new to you. if I let it, this could be home.
maybe you could be home.

in which we watch my words burn

I wish I could tell you what this night means
to me; lying next to you next to the fire,
under the august stars. and I wish I could tell you
how it felt to burn old poems written by inexperienced hands,
written about high school crushes and never feeling good
enough. to watch angst and embarrassment crumble
into ash.
I didn't know what I was doing then, pen on paper / incoherent
scribbles. the words inside me needed to come out, but
I didn't know how to turn them into poetry.
            they remained hidden for so long. I don't let you look
            at them before I throw them into the flames.
I poke at them with a stick and the embers dance around us
till they vanish. erased. inexistent.
I wrote of heartbreak without knowing what love was. now
I do.
I wish I could tell you how this feels, but there's no word for the
aftermath
of those burning pages and knowing I'm good enough
for you and for the world. knowing that I'm safe with you.
so I listen to your heartbeat and stare up at the embers, flaming
stars
fading against an indigo night.
I let this be enough.

in which our new year's kiss is at 3pm

you tell me not to worry, you'll drive safe. I know
there is money to be made, drinks to be poured
to be spilled on beer garden benches. the snow suffocates
all sound but the crunch of my boots
through thick ice and packed snowfall. I worry:
about you driving over ice
about you spinning out
about your car under a semi, aluminum accordion.

     right on cue, you text me: *here safe.*
     I miss you.

what do you fear? do you worry like me –
forced breath and tight chest and film-reel-thoughts
spiraling through your mind? I worry
that I worry too much. do you hate this?
do you love me? I sleep alone tonight.
in your absence, you join me in dreams.

     at midnight, you text me: *happy new year.*
     I love you.

in which I bake banana bread as a gift

outside, the mountains are obscured
by thick smoke – choked
by wildfires – the sun a scarlet orb descending
through ash. inside, I balance myself
on a stool – moving boxes half-unpacked, stacked
– against bare walls – folding chocolate chips
and hastily-chopped walnuts into the batter.
it has been thirty-seven days
since the surgery that removed an unidentifiable foreign object
from the sole of my foot. *(I think it was a glass shard; you think
it was a cactus spike.)* I struggle to perform
this simple act of baking, each step uneasy and
stilted, like wading in molasses. tenderly dragging
my aching foot behind me
to the oven
to bake this offering.
it has been thirty-seven days
since I didn't feel like a burden: unable to walk
without pain or shower on my own, struggling
up stairs as you patiently wait.
food is my love language, the only way I can thank you.

in which you travel by plane for the first time

you take the window seat. my hands grip armrests,
white-knuckled and shaking as we take off.
I dread the weightlessness, heart in my throat;
wheels on pavement at 130 miles per hour,

bones shaking in my skin. I prefer to close my eyes,
but I watch you as we ascend. have I ever seen you smile
like this? youthful wonder as we fly over the mountains,
over our home. you point out landmarks – mount baker –

the refinery – seattle – as evergreen mountains transform
into rolling hills of yellowing grass. you marvel
at the world below for 900 miles, and I smile
through my fear, let your elation calm me.

in which we get drunk in a las vegas speakeasy

I am already a little drunk, and you are already thirty,
but I raise my glass and toast to you – happy birthday.

we solved puzzles in a safe and crawled through holes
behind crates, found ourselves in a dimly-lit room,

holes in portrait eyes. we filled out questionnaires on the backs
of coasters (me: pisces, beach, sweet, no tequila / you: scorpio,

beach, savory, bourbon). I am in love with this moment,
intoxicated by it. you glance at me and all I can think about

is how you have lived three decades and I have known you
for less than one. I feel as if I've known you for the entirety

of our lives. I wonder if there is a word for this – this feeling
of knowing another so intimately that this knowing

transcends time. how lucky I am to have this knowing.
I want to climb on the table, declare how it has felt to love

you for 2,841 days to the entire room. to give you so much
more than a toast in a las vegas speakeasy. but I am already

a little drunk, and I can tell by the way you look at me
that you already know. that you love me with the same knowing.

in which we sit by the campfire all night

we sit in comfortable silence, enchanted by the flames.
the sky grows darker, the stars brighter, pinpricks
of brilliance in midnight canvas.
my skin: a sponge.
>I feel glacial water in my bones, echo
>of our afternoon swim in the mountainside lake.
>I feel your breath on my neck, bodies entwined
>on hard ground under morning sunlight.
>I feel the touch of your lips on my own,
>warm and tender under towering trees.

disconnected
from everyone but each other.
imagine living in this moment for eternity,
warmed by the glow of the fire,
the melody of birdsong through leaves
and bugs chirping our daily soundtrack.
I never want to return home
if it means I can stay with you in these woods,
uninterrupted and in love forever.

in which you decide to quit your job

your breaking point comes after three-hundred
and seventy-five days of chaos. how long has it been
since we spent a night uninterrupted? how long
has it been since you were happy? when you speak,
there is no hope in your voice.
I have been trailing behind you, picking up
the pieces chipped away, gluing seams
with gold; I don't know how to fix a spirit, completely
shattered. I wish I had the words
to give you, could hand them over gently, wrapped
and clean. instead, they are clumsy
on my tongue. you don't have room for my anger.
I am not soft. I am sorry for this. but I ask you now – do you
know
this is not failure? do you know how strong you are?
do you know how much I love you?

in which I cry at the boygenius concert

picture this: the columbia river snakes
through the valley, stained purple/green
/red by stage lights. tears trickle down
flushed cheeks. I don't wipe them away.
(do you notice them, glistening in the stars?)

picture this: I sing too loud to feel
alive; touch the ground with electric
fingertips; the bass reverberates
through my bones, shakes my soul.
(do you feel it, too?)

picture this: I have had too much
to drink and the band is playing
my favorite song and I love you so
much and I'm trying to be cool about it.
(am I being cool about it?)

picture this: the promise of a thousand
lifetimes with you is intoxicatingly
overwhelming. if I only get one lifetime
with you, I am grateful for this one.
for this moment. (are you, too?)

in which I compose a love letter

do you remember the way the mid-morning sun crept through the blinds of your basement apartment, the one I moved into that spring? so many days, I woke before you and admired the sunlight illuminating your face. I have memorized you: the sharp ridge of your nose, each hair on your face, your maple-syrup eyes. I could be away from you for centuries and never forget each detail. love has etched you onto my soul forever.

one morning, I looked at you and tried to remember the first time I said *I love you* – a lifetime of giving *I love you* and a lifetime of receiving it has clouded my memory. in that moment, I felt such guilt. should I remember? should this memory be as clear in my mind as your likeness?

maybe.

but I remember that day by the lake: my head on your shoulder under the warm spring sun. we rested after a hike, sore and sweaty. your voice echoed through the trees, rolled across the water, and I swear I could see ripples where your laugh skipped across the surface. in that moment, I realized I loved you. I have never stopped.

your laughter still shakes the water. we're still together in the sunlight.

acknowledgements

Mom & Dad – for everything. but most importantly, for never discouraging me from writing. I hope I always make you proud.

Sarah – for reading these poems and writing such sweet words about them. I am thankful to know you as a writer, but most thankful to know you as a friend.

Cindy – for being my number one fan and reading every word I write.

Uncle Dan – for always encouraging me to keep writing.

Willow – for being the greatest editor in the world, and the best cat.

and, of course, Tre – the love of my life, my best friend. I am thankful for every moment with you, and look forward to a million more.

notes

in which we watch my words burn was previously published by Poetically Mag (as "untitled love poem, in which we watch my words burn")

about the author

katherine j zumpano is a poet and writer in the pacific northwest. she lives with her partner of seven years and their cat, willow. she received her BA in creative writing from Western Washington University, and daydreams about going back to school to earn her MA. her work has been published in Jeopardy Magazine, Southchild Lit, and more.

Printed in the USA
CPSIA information can be obtained
at www.ICGtesting.com
CBHW050806061223
2379CB00029B/203